Whose Feet Are These?
A Look at Hooves, Paws, and Claws

Written by Peg Hall

Illustrated by Ken Landmark

Content Advisor: Julie Dunlap, Ph.D.

Reading Advisor: Lauren A. Liang, M.A.

Literacy Education, University of Minnesota, Minneapolis, Minnesota

PICTURE WINDOW BOOKS
Minneapolis, Minnesota

Editor: Lisa Morris Kee
Designer: Melissa Voda
Page production: The Design Lab
The illustrations in this book were prepared digitally.

Printed in the United States of America.

Library of Congress Cataloging-in-Publication Data
Hall, Peg.
  Whose feet are these? : a look at hooves, paws, and claws / written by Peg Hall;
illustrated by Ken Landmark.
    p. cm. — (Whose is it?)
Summary: Examines a variety of animal feet, noting how they look different and
function in different ways.
  ISBN 1-4048-0006-9 (lib. bdg. : alk. paper)
  1. Foot—Juvenile literature. [1. Foot. 2. Animals.] I. Landmark, Ken, ill. II. Title.
QL950.7 .H34 2003
591.47'9—dc21   2002005775

Picture Window Books
5115 Excelsior Boulevard
Suite 232
Minneapolis, MN 55416
1-877-845-8392
www.picturewindowbooks.com

Here's a clue to tell who's who.

Look closely at an animal's feet. Feet can be hard, soft, round, or pointed. Some feet are webbed, and others have claws.

How feet look can tell you many things. Feet can tell you if an animal digs, swims, climbs, or hops. Feet can tell you whether an animal lives in a rainy jungle or a dry desert. There are even feet that help animals taste their food.

Feet don't all look alike, because they don't all work alike.

Let's look at some neat feet.

Look in the back for more fun facts about feet.

4

Whose feet are these, paddling in the water?

These are a duck's feet.

A duck has webbed feet. Skin stretches between each of its long front toes. Webbed feet help the duck paddle quickly through water.

Fun fact: A duck has three toes pointing forward and one tiny toe pointing backward. The front toes are spread out to make the duck's webbed foot extra wide.

Whose feet are these, balancing on a rock?

7

These are a mountain goat's hooves.

A mountain goat jumps from one steep slope to another. Rough pads on the bottom of each hoof keep it from slipping. Even a baby goat can grip a slippery slope.

Fun fact: A mountain goat's hooves are split into two big toes. The goat can spread its toes apart to hold on to rocks.

Whose feet are these, digging in the dark?

9

These are a mole's feet.

The mole is digging a tunnel. Its long claws loosen the dirt. The mole's big front feet work like shovels to scoop the dirt and move it out of the way.

Fun fact: Moles don't have toes. Their claws come straight out of their feet.

Whose feet are these, reaching for a clam?

These are a starfish's feet.

The starfish has hundreds of feet on each of its arms. The feet are hollow tubes with powerful suckers at the ends. A starfish sticks its feet onto a clamshell and pulls it open.

Fun fact: A starfish pumps water in and out of its body. That makes its feet lengthen and bend so it can walk.

Whose feet are these, holding a stick?

13

These are a chimpanzee's feet.

A chimpanzee walks on its feet, just like you do. But it can also use its feet like hands to pick up and hold things. Each foot has four long toes that look like fingers and one toe that moves like a thumb.

Fun fact: Chimpanzees live in forests. Their strong feet are just right for climbing trees and jumping quickly from branch to branch.

Whose feet are these, climbing a tree?

These are a cougar's paws.

A cougar sneaks up on its prey. Its sharp claws hide inside its toes. When the cougar attacks, the claws spring out.

Fun fact: If a cougar's claws get dull, the cougar sharpens them by scratching a tree trunk.

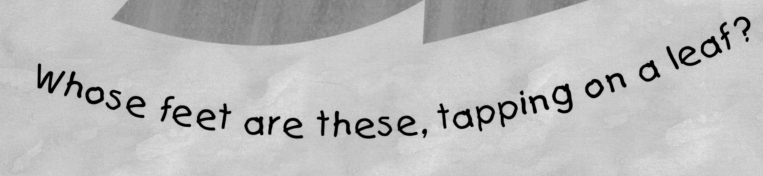

Whose feet are these, tapping on a leaf?

These are a butterfly's feet.

The butterfly can taste a leaf with its feet.
If the leaf has the right taste, the
butterfly may lay her eggs on it.

Fun fact: You taste your food with tiny bumps on your tongue. The butterfly tastes with special hairs on its feet.

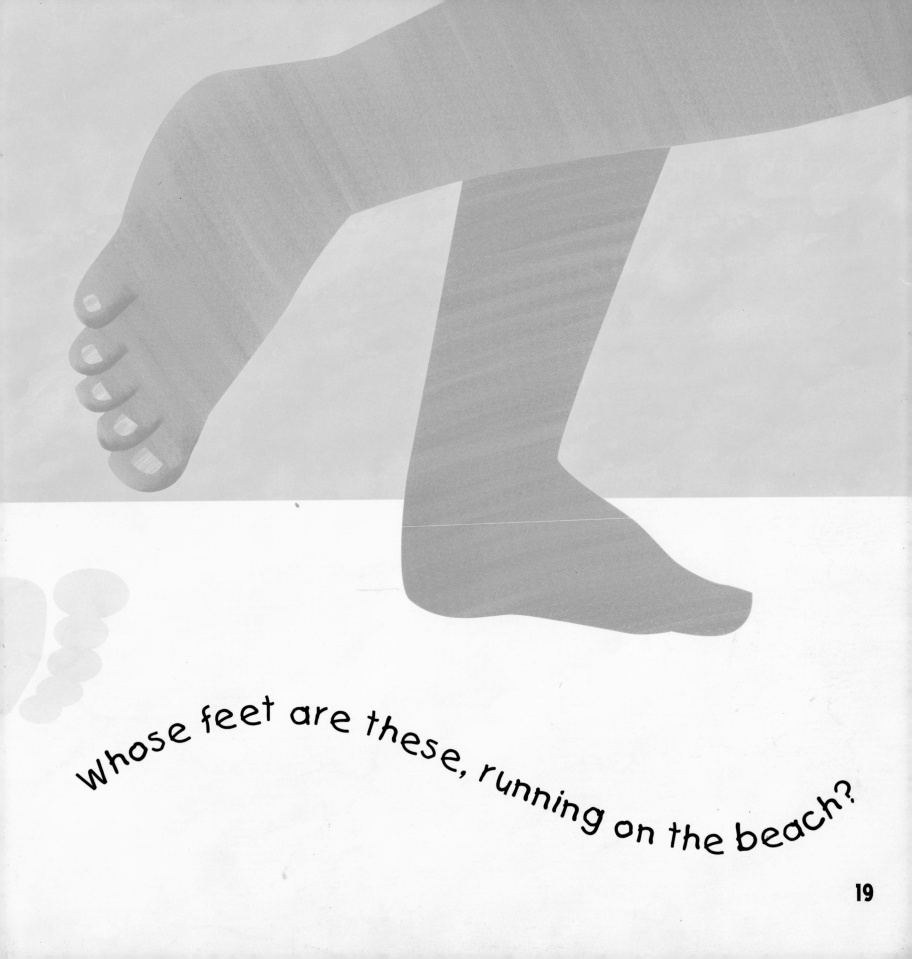

Whose feet are these, running on the beach?

These are your feet!

Your feet are just right for walking, running, kicking a ball, or standing on tiptoe. What else do your feet do?

You have toenails where some animals have claws. If your feet were webbed, would you swim like a duck? If you had the feet of a chimpanzee, would you climb a tree and hunt for bananas?

Just for Fun

Can you answer these riddles about feet?

I have feet on my arms. Who am I?

I am a starfish.

I use my feet like shovels. Who am I?

I am a mole.

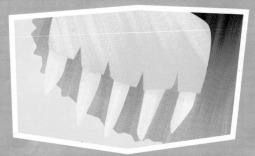

My feet are like paddles. Who am I?

I am a duck.

Fun Facts About Feet

WIDE FEET The camel spreads its toes out when it walks on sand. The spreading toes stretch the foot wide. Extra-wide feet keep the camel from sinking into the sand.

SNEAKY FEET Cats walk on their toes. All cats have a thick pad under each toe. The pads let cats walk very quietly. Lions, cougars, and house cats can all walk in the same quiet way.

SHARP FEET The hawk has three sharp toes that curve forward, and one toe that curves back. The hawk squeezes its front and back toes together to grab its prey.

DIGGING FEET The mole cricket has huge front feet. It uses its feet like shovels to dig in the dirt, just like a mole does.

CLEAN FEET Some animals use their feet to help them stay clean. The beaver combs its fur with special claws on its hind feet. Cats lick their front paws and use them like washcloths to clean their faces and behind their ears.

TASTY FEET Butterflies, houseflies, and bees are all insects that taste their food with their feet.

FURRY FEET A polar bear has thick fur on its paws, even on the bottoms. The fur keeps the bear from slipping on ice. It also makes the bear's steps quiet as it sneaks up on its prey.

Words to Know

claws Claws are sharp, curved toenails.

hooves Hooves are the hard coverings on the feet of some animals.

suckers Suckers are parts of an animal's foot that stick to things.

paws The feet of animals with four feet and claws are called paws.

prey Prey are animals that are hunted and eaten by other animals.

To Learn More

AT THE LIBRARY

Schwartz, David M. **Animal Feet.** Milwaukee,
  Wis.: Gareth Stevens, 2000.

Selsam, Millicent Ellis. **Big Tracks, Little
  Tracks: Following Animal Prints.**
  New York: HarperCollins, 1999.

Swanson, Diane. **Feet That Suck and Feed.**
  Vancouver: Greystone Books, 2000.

ON THE WEB

Lincoln Park Zoo
http://www.lpzoo.com
Explore the animals at the Lincoln Park Zoo.

San Diego Zoo
http://www.sandiegozoo.org
Learn about animals and their habitats.

Want to learn more about animal feet?
Visit FACT HOUND at
http://www.facthound.com

Index